LIFESTYLE ARCHITECTURE

AFFINITI ARCHITECTS

AFFINITI
ARCHITECTS

LIFESTYLE ARCHITECTURE

TIMELESS DESIGNS FOR GENERATIONS

ORO

ORO Editions, Novato, California

CONTENTS

THE BOOK

As demonstrated by the homes selected for this publication, Affiniti Architects works in multiple architectural styles. This is a result of teamwork with builders, developers, investors, realtors, designers, engineers, subcontractors, existing clients, and new clients.

Affiniti's philosophy of timeless design creates the backdrop that is developed by site, massing, style, views, entry, indoor/outdoor, detail, and open spaces. The key to a successful design is a thoughtful response to the location of a residence and the needs for living in the home.

The photos, drawings, and renderings in this book captures the variety of methods and ideas which can be created and brought to reality. Consistency within each project is an overwhelming focus unifying all aspects of the process. Having a love of architecture to is key to the beautiful and timeless homes shown in this book.

We are only as good as the last home designed. Affiniti keeps moving forward, giving everyone involved space for creativity, passion, and collaboration.

AFFINITI
architects

THE FIRM

Affiniti's exemplary design reputation over the last 40 years has been recognized with over three hundred and fifty industry design awards. Homes have been featured in numerous regional and national architectural publications. With work totaling over $30 Billion, the firm's architectural influences can be seen throughout the United States, Caribbean, Central America, and overseas.

Our greatest goal, philosophy, and attribute is fulfilling our client's dreams. Most of our work is with discerning clients who often come back to us with their next best-dream projects. Affiniti prides itself in creating legacy architecture for generations which is beautiful, has thoughtful details and endures the test of time.

Our task does not end until the client is moved into their home and completely happy. One-of-a-kind architectural designs utilizing a combination of clients, design team and builders' input, with conceptual images allows infinite possibilities fitting many lifestyles.

BUT I'M ALWAYS AROUND
SLOW DOWN...
ENJOY...
BREATHE...
AIN'T IT COOL WHAT WE DID?
KISSES BJK

TEAM

OUR GREATEST
INSPIRATION, PHILOSOPHY,
AND ATTRIBUTE
IS THE FULFILLMENT
OF OUR CLIENT'S DREAM.

SITE

DESIGN WITH CONTEXT

SEASIDE TREEHOUSE

LEGACY ESTATE

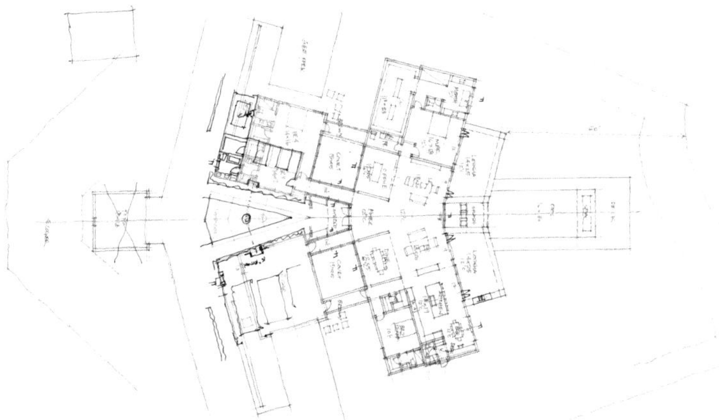

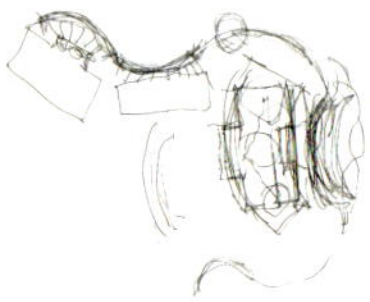

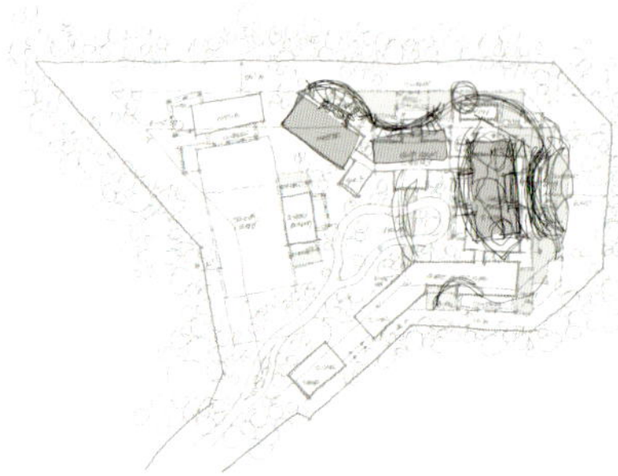

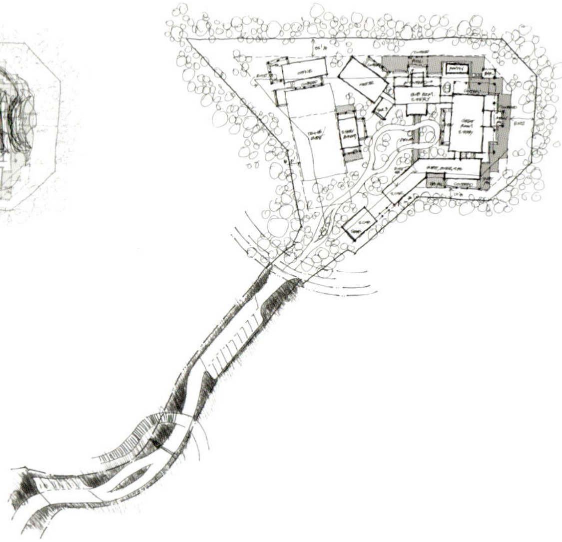

FAIRWAY MANOR

TUSCAN MEDITERRANEAN

[RIGHT]
MID-CENTURY MODERN

1271

WEST INDIES CIRCLE

[RIGHT]
PACIFIC MODERN

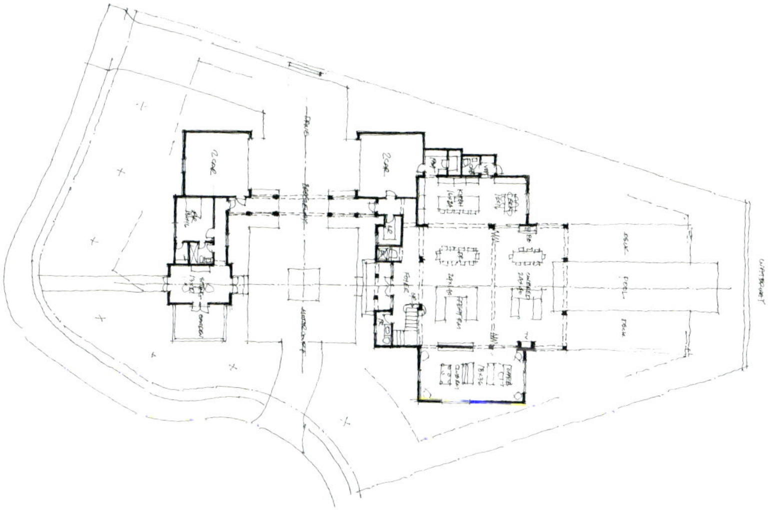

[LEFT]
OCEANSIDE MODERN

WATERSIDE CONTEMPORARY

PACIFIC MODERN

[RIGHT]
RUSTIC CARIBBEAN ESTATE

COURTYARD CONTEMPORARY

MASSING

FIRST IMPRESSIONS

INTRACOASTAL CONTEMPO

PACIFIC MODERN

[LEFT]
WEST INDIES CAY

MARTINI HOUSE

NEO CLASSICAL SYMMETRY

COURTYARD CONTEMPORARY

[RIGHT]
COASTAL FARMHOUSE

FLAGLER CONTEMPORARY

[LEFT]
MODERN ON THE GREENS

[RIGHT]
OLD PALM MODERN

[BELOW]
5TH AVENUE ENCLAVE

CONTEMPORARY LOFT

STYLE

TIMELESS LEGACY ARCHITECTURE

CLASSIC MEDITERRANEAN

COURTYARD CONTEMPORARY

[LEFT]
MARTINI HOUSE

COASTAL FARMHOUSE

WEST INDIES CIRCLE

5TH AVENUE ENCLAVE

[RIGHT]
SOUTH WEST RANCHES BALINESE MODELS

Contemporary Model
Modern Model
Island Model

TRANSITIONAL OCEANFRONT

[LEFT]
SEASIDE TREEHOUSE

TRANSITIONAL OCEANFRONT

[BELOW]
SEASIDE CARIBBEAN

DUTCH WEST INDIES

PACIFIC MODERN

[RIGHT]
MID CENTURY MODERN

1271

[LEFT]
RIVERSIDE WEST INDIES

CARIBBEAN PALM

[BELOW]
RUSTIC COVE

TRANSITIONAL BAY

[RIGHT]
ISLE CONTEMPORARY

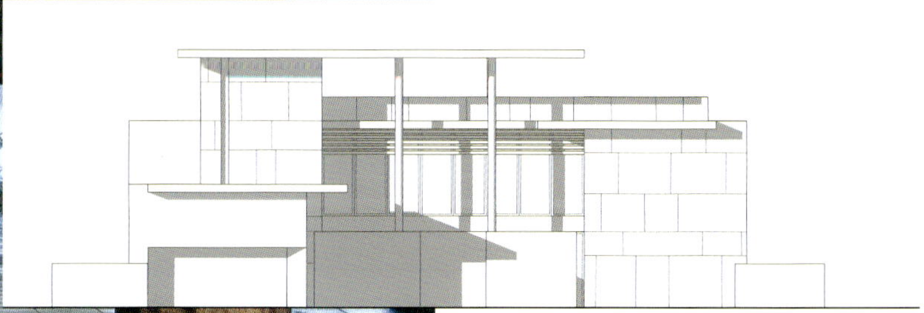

MODERN RIVIERA

VIEWS

BEYOND THE LOOKING GLASS

NAUTICAL BREEZE

PACIFIC MODERN

[BELOW]
CONTEMPORARY LOFT

[RIGHT]
INTRACOASTAL CONTEMPO

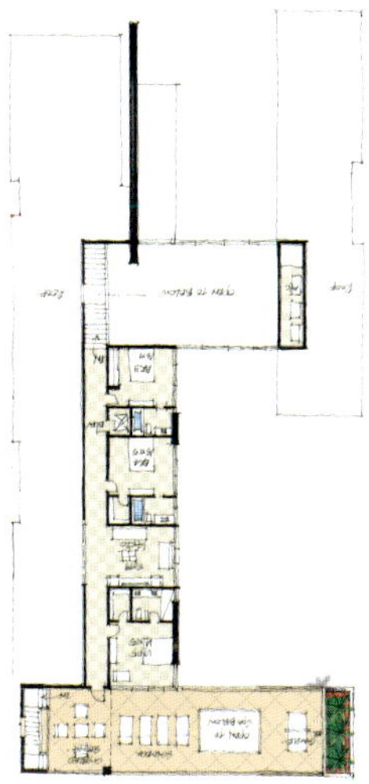

5TH AVENUE ENCLAVE

[LEFT]
CONTEMPORARY RIO

MARTINI HOUSE

[BELOW]
ISLE CONTEMPORARY

WATERSIDE TRANSITIONAL

[BELOW]
HARBOR CONTEMPORARY

[RIGHT]
DUTCH WEST INDIES

COURTYARD CONTEMPORARY

ENTRY

WELCOMING MOMENT

NAUTICAL BREEZE

MODERN ANDREWS

[LEFT]
CONTEMPORARY HILLSBORO

WEST INDIES CIRCLE

[LEFT]
MID-CENTURY MODERN

WATERFRONT MARINER

[RIGHT]
MARTINI HOUSE

MODERN WATERWAY

DUTCH WEST INDIES

[RIGHT]
CONTEMPORARY LOFT

5TH AVENUE ENCLAVE

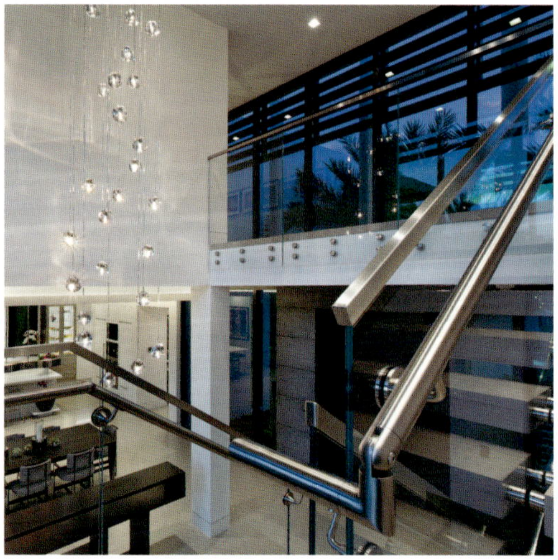

CARIBBEAN GULF

[BELOW]
CONTEMPORARY RANCH

ISLE CONTEMPORARY

[LEFT]
CLASSIC MEDITERRANEAN

WEST INDIES CIRCLE

MODERN EVERGREEN

1325

OUTSIDE IN

LIVING IN PARADISE

RIVERSIDE WEST INDIES

5TH AVENUE ENCLAVE

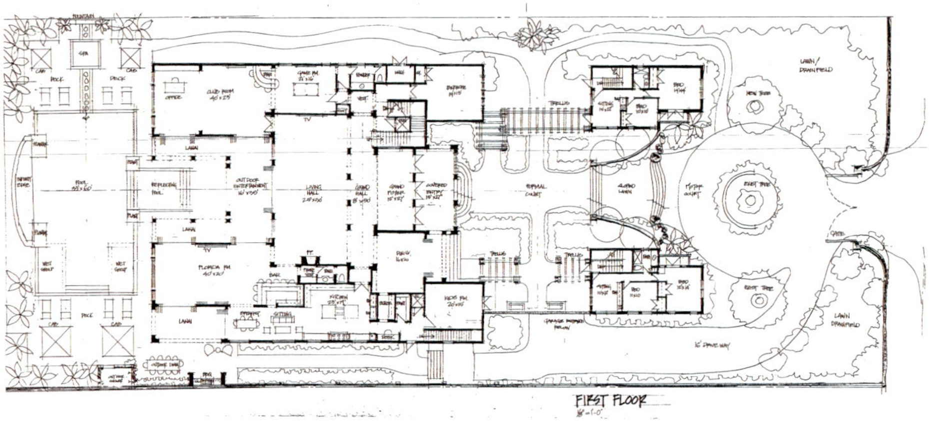

SEASIDE TREEHOUSE

RUSTIC CARIBBEAN ESTATE

[BELOW]
RUSTIC COVE

[RIGHT]
MID-CENTURY MODERN

NYSE

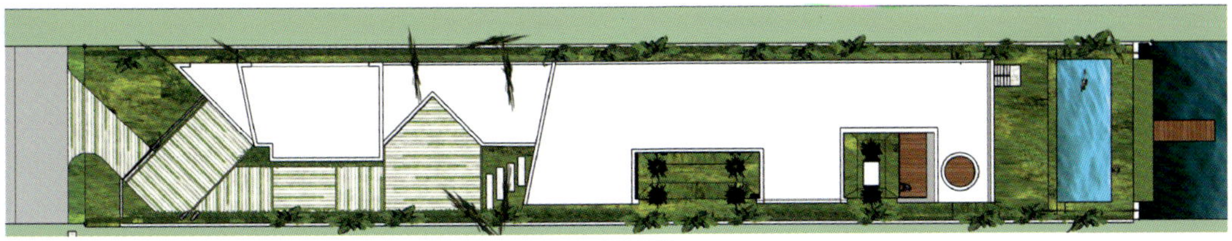

ROOF PLAN

GROUND FLOOR PLAN

SECOND FLOOR PLAN

6TH AVENUE ENCLAVE

ISLE CONTEMPORARY

RUSTIC CARIBBEAN ESTATE

[RIGHT]
DUTCH WEST INDIES

[BELOW]
INTRACOASTAL PEARL

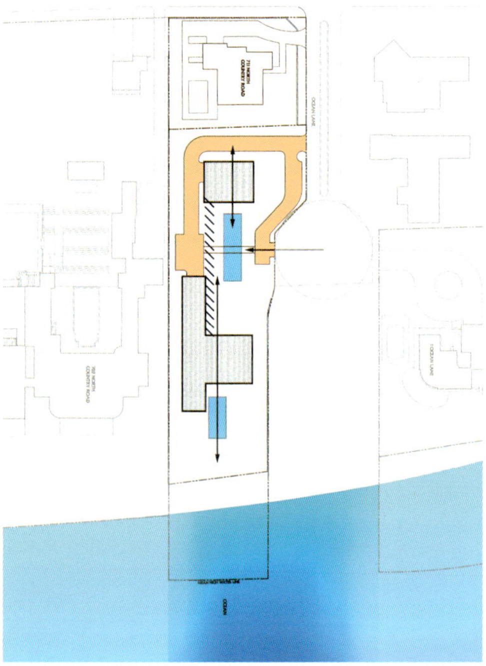

COURTYARD CONTEMPORARY

[LEFT]
OCEANFRONT PALM BEACH

COURTYARD CONTEMPORARY

[BELOW]
SABAL PALM

SPACES

YOUR HAPPY PLACE

LAKESIDE TRANSITIONAL

CONTEMPORARY LOFT

[BELOW]
SEASIDE TREEHOUSE

[RIGHT]
CONTEMPORARY RANCH

COURTYARD CONTEMPORARY

DUTCH WEST INDIES

COUNTRY PALM ROYALTON
MODEL

SABAL PALM

[RIGHT]
WATERWAY
CONTEMPORARY LAKE

5TH AVENUE ENCLAVE

[RIGHT]
CLASSIC MEDITERRANEAN

[LEFT]
INTRACOASTAL CONTEMPO

DUTCH WEST INDIES

[BELOW]
TRANSITIONAL FAIRWAYS

RUSTIC COVE

[RIGHT]
TRANSITIONAL FAIRWAYS

[LEFT]
CONTEMPORARY RIO

[BELOW]
PACIFIC MODERN

RIVERSIDE WEST INDIES

MODERN WATERWAY

British West Indies Style
SCULPTURE

DETAILS

ARCHITECTURE IS LIKE AN AIRPLANE WING
SO IT NEEDS TO BE FLEXIBLE

DUTCH WEST INDIES

5TH AVENUE ENCLAVE

[LEFT]
MODERN ANDREWS

WEST INDIES CIRCLE

[BELOW]
MODERN ON THE GREENS

MARTINI HOUSE

WEST INDIES CIRCLE

DUTCH WEST INDIES

[RIGHT]
COURTYARD CONTEMPORARY

[LEFT]
MARTINI HOUSE

WATERSIDE
CONTEMPORARY

RUSTIC COVE

[LEFT]
DUTCH WEST INDIES

[RIGHT]
TRANSITIONAL CARIBBEAN

[LEFT]
5TH AVENUE ENCLAVE

[RIGHT]
TRANSITIONAL CARIBBEAN

MODERN ON THE GREENS

[BELOW]
TRANSITIONAL CARIBBEAN

[RIGHT]
CLASSIC MEDITERRANEAN

SEASIDE TREEHOUSE

[RIGHT]
TROPICAL RUSTIC

WEST INDIES ESTATE

[BELOW]
CONTEMPORARY TRANSITIONAL

6'-0"

[LEFT]
CLASSIC MEDITERRANEAN

SEASIDE TREEHOUSE

WATERWAY VIEWS

IN THE OPEN

SUN & SHADE IN HARMONY

WEST INDIES ESTATE

MID CENTURY MODERN

CONTEMPORARY
TRANSITIONAL

[RIGHT]
ISLE CONTEMPORARY

[LEFT]
PACIFIC MODERN

[BELOW]
FAIRWAY MANOR

MARTINI HOUSE

MODERN EVERGREEN

[RIGHT]
COURTYARD CONTEMPORARY

[BELOW]
RIVERSIDE WEST INDIES

[LEFT]
DUTCH WEST INDIES

5TH AVENUE ENCLAVE

WATERVIEW CONTEMPORARY

[RIGHT]
NAUTICAL BREEZE

ISLAND COLONIAL ESTATE

[BELOW]
TRANSITIONAL CARIBBEAN

[RIGHT]
COURTYARD CONTEMPORARY

MODERN ANDREWS

WE LOOK FORWARD
TO THE NEXT 40 YEARS
OF CREATING
TIMELESS LEGACY ARCHITECTURE
FOR GENERATIONS.

ACKNOWLEGEMENT

The success of any business is a team effort, Affiniti would like to express our sincere appreciation to founding partner Mitchell F. Kunik, partners Benjamin M. Schreier, Matthew W. Wheeler, Huy D. Nguyen and partner-emeritus Brian Collins. Special thanks to our clients for their trust, support, and confidence in our firm to design and be part of our custom, builders, and investors dream homes.

We appreciate our current, past, and future professionals at Affiniti for their dedication, hard work, and passion for architecture. To our families, friends, and loved ones, we express our deepest gratitude for your understanding, patience, and continuous support. You are all an inspiration to us.

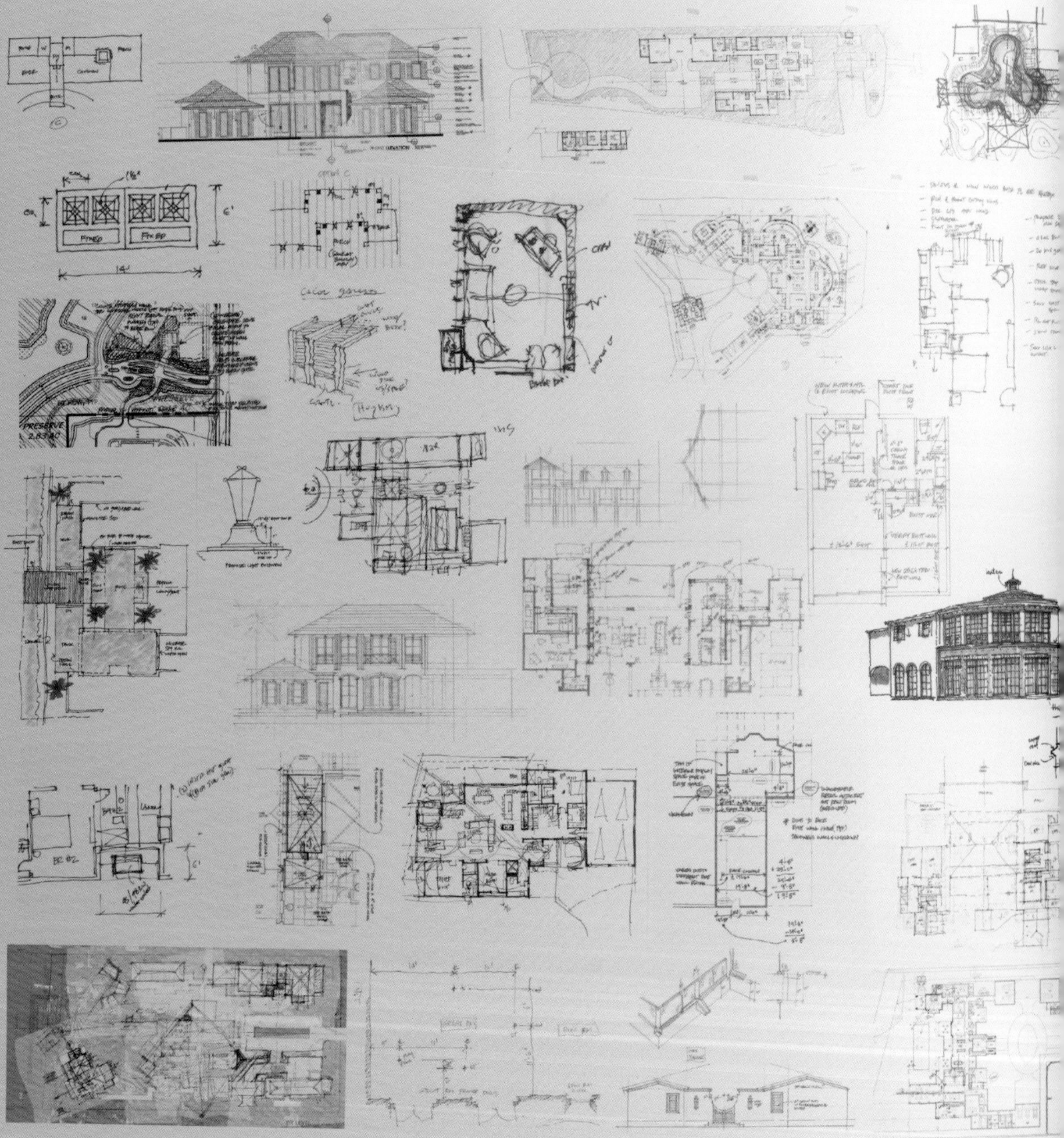
PRESERVE

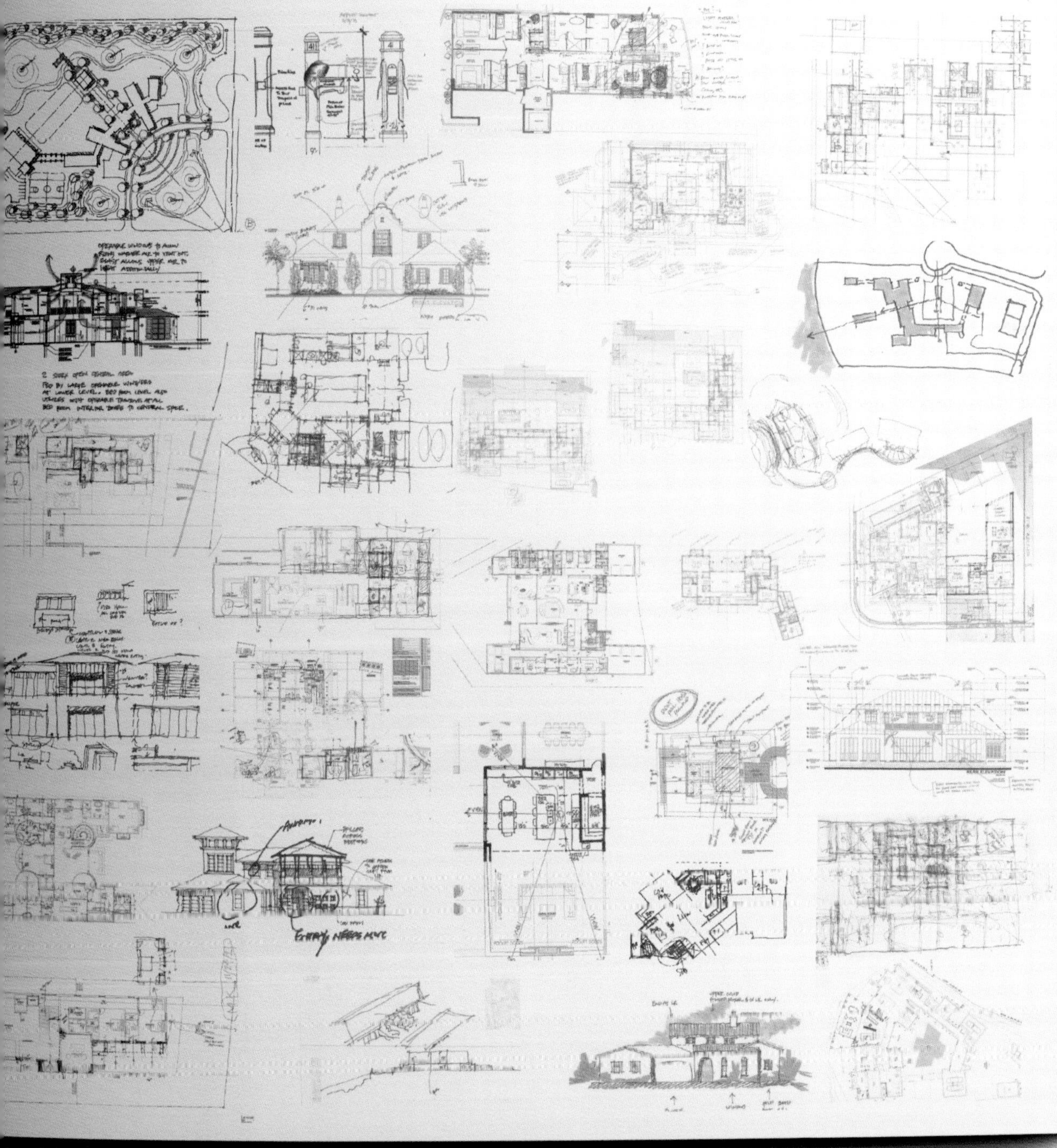

CREDENTIALS

BUILDERS & DEVELOPERS

Turtle Beach Construction
Mark Timothy INC
Courchene Development
National Custom Homes
Onshore Construction & Development INC
Bloomfield Construction
Landmark Estates
D. Garrett Construction
Shapiro Pertnoy
Wadsworth Developers
AVI Contractors INC
Cudmore Builders
Hobgood Construction
Coastal Properties
KMR Construction
STAG Development
Summit Builders
Bomar Builders
Ellemar Luxury Construction
Ark Residential Corp
Affinity Builders
Alonso Associates

LANDSCAPE ARCHITECTS

KWD Landscape Architecture
Lang Design Group
Peterson Design Professionals
Parker-Yannette Design Group
Anthony Sciortino
Windham Studios INC
Gill Design Group
Majestic View Landscape
Nievera Williams Design
Don Murakami
PK Design Studio
DS Boca
PLA Design Studio
Insite Studio

INTERIOR DESIGNERS

Marc Michaels Interiors
The Decorators Unlimited
Erin A Cantu Interiors Inc
Interiors Michele Osborn Design Heidi Maya
Steven G Interiors
Jill H. Crompton with Hepworth Designs
Louis Anthony & Associates Inc
Shuster Design Associates, INC
Scott Snyder INC
Lesly Maxwell Interiors Inc
Terri Polimeni Interiors
J R Design

PHOTOGRAPHERS

Andy Frame Photography

Andy Ziffer Photography

Brantley Photography

Carlos Domenech Photography

Daniel Newcomb Photography

Danny Petroni Photography

IBI Designs

Jack Bates Photography

Living Proof Photography

Mike Butler Photography

Pelican Pix Photography

Ron Rosenzweig Photography

Sargent Photography

Tom Knibbs Photography

Troy Campbell Photography

CONTRIBUTORS

Duane Addy

ENGINEERS

Structural

Project Classic

Delta G

Brennan Engineering

Kuhn Engineering

Unison Structural Design LLC

Schulke, Bittle & Stoddard

ONMJ Structural Engineers

Mechanical

JWL Engineering

Iced Engineering

Tom Henz, INC.

LIFESTYLE
ARCHITECTURE
AFFINITI
ARCHITECTS

ORO Editions
Publishers of Architecture, Art, and Design
Gordon Goff: Publisher

www.oroeditions.com
info@oroeditions.com

Published by ORO Editions

Typeset in TT Hoves and Avant Garde

Graphic Design: Shanean Lee Hue / Affiniti Architects with Pablo Mandel / CircularStudio
ORO Project Coordinator: Kirby Anderson

10 9 8 7 6 5 4 3 2 1 First Edition

Library of Congress data available upon request. World Rights: Available

ISBN: 978-1-954081-91-8

Color Separations and Printing: ORO Group Ltd.
Printed in China.

International Distribution: www.oroeditions.com/distribution

ORO Editions makes a continuous effort to minimize the overall carbon footprint of its publications. As part of this goal, ORO Editions, in association with Global ReLeaf, arranges to plant trees to replace those used in the manufacturing of the paper produced for its books. Global ReLeaf is an international campaign run by American Forests, one of the world's oldest nonprofit conservation organizations. Global ReLeaf is American Forests' education and action program that helps individuals, organizations, agencies, and corporations improve the local and global environment by planting and caring for trees.